better together*

*This book is best read together, grownup and kid.

 akidsco.com

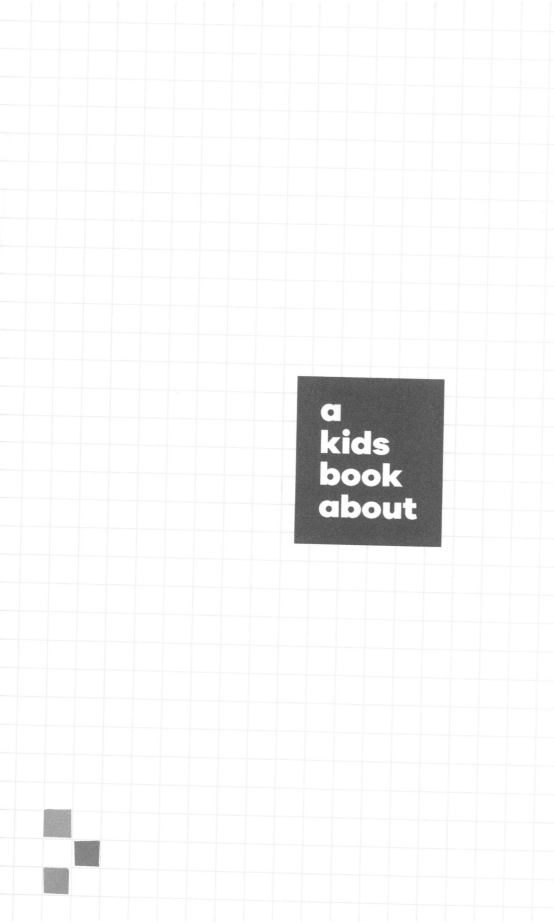

a
kids
book
about

a kids book about

SCHOOL

by Rachel Burger

a kids book about

Printed in the United States of America.

A Kids Book About books are available online: *akidsco.com*

To share your stories, ask questions, or inquire about bulk purchases (schools, libraries, and nonprofits), please use the following email address: *hello@akidsco.com*

Print ISBN: 978-1-958825-73-0
Ebook ISBN: 978-1-958825-74-7

Designed by Rick DeLucco
Edited by Emma Wolf

For 2 loves of my life, Jacob and Miles, and every class I've had the privilege of teaching and loving. You teach me so much every day, and I hope you enjoy a lifetime of learning.

For my fellow teachers: despite the challenges we face, may we continue to shine a light on the power of learning and guide our students toward it.

intro

 hy do we go to school? Why do we have grades? How did school start and become the way it is?

These are all questions I have been asked as a teacher. (Students have the best questions about school!) It is great to be curious and want to know why you are doing something— clear signs that you are ready for school!

People have all sorts of feelings about school: they like it, they don't; it's hard, it's easy; and more. This book answers some questions you may have about school, but will also get you thinking about the power school has to help you grow and learn.

Going to school may not always feel fun. But it's a place to explore, discover, make connections, make mistakes, and become the version of yourself you love most.

Hi! I'm RACHEL.

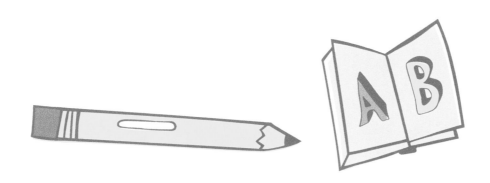

I'm a teacher, and I work in a school.

You might already be in school, or maybe you're about to go to school for the first time.

WHEN YOU THINK OF SCHOOL, WHAT COMES TO MIND?

Is it a place where you go, sit, and listen to someone talk all day?

It's a little bit like that (sometimes), but school is also so much more.

I think of school kind of like a

GARDEN.

Just like plants need water, nutrients, and sun to grow big and strong, school is where our brains grow, stretch, and get stronger.

School is where you

DISCOVER
THINGS

you like, and things you don't like.

School is where you

CAN MAKE
CONNECTIONS

with new people and good friends.

Even as a teacher, I still learn new things about myself and the people around me when I go to school!

Now, I know school isn't always everyone's favorite place to be.

SO, WHY DO WE NEED IT?

School teaches us the basics of how to do things and how the world works.

It helps us learn...

TO EXPLORE
OUR INTERESTS.

HOW TO CREATE SOLUTIONS TO PROBLEMS,

TO COMMUNICATE WITH OTHER PEOPLE,

AND TO BE PATIENT ☮ WITH THINGS WE DON'T LIKE.

You see, school isn't just math, science, and history classes.

It's where you build relationships, learn problem-solving skills, and other things you'll need for the rest of your life.

When you go to school,
you'll probably receive a grade*
for the different work you do.

*A grade is a score for how you did in your school work.
Sometimes you'll see them in numbers (like a scale
from 1–4 or 1-100%), sometimes they'll be written as pass/
fail, and sometimes you'll see them in letters (A, B, C, D, or F).

Grades aren't meant to be judgments on you and they don't say anything about you as a whole person.

SO, WHY DO WE USE THEM IN SCHOOL?

Grades are meant to show you and your teachers areas in which you are doing well, as well as areas where you might need some extra help.

I know when students don't get the grades they want, that can feel bad. I've been there too!

IT'S SUPER NORMAL

and it's important for you to remember that *you* are not bad.

We all have areas we need to keep growing in, things we're maybe not the best at, and that's **OK.**

Imagine if everyone was good at only one thing.

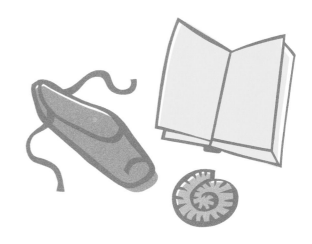

We might have a million doctors, but then we wouldn't have anybody who could teach dance classes, write books, study fossils, do construction work, or be professional athletes.

Everybody is good at different things, and that's what makes our world work!

 so...

HOW
DID
SCHOOL
START?

In its early years, school was only available based on things like race, gender, income, or location.

Basically, it was a privilege, not a right.

There weren't standards like there are today, so teaching was organized based on what the community thought was best.

Parents, religious leaders, private tutors—many different people taught kids.

But it became clear that to live in a democratic society where the people can make choices and become government leaders, we all need to be informed about certain issues.

After the American Revolution, we worked to establish a more uniform school system.

Eventually, a good and fair education was prioritized as a need for all kids.

THINGS LOOK BETTER NOW, BUT IT DOESN'T MEAN SCHOOL IS PERFECT.

There are many things that need to improve.

There are still communities that don't have access to quality education:

people with less money, people with diverse cultural backgrounds, kids with special needs (to name a few).

In some countries, girls aren't even allowed to go to school.

THAT DOESN'T SOUND FAIR, RIGHT?

IT'S NOT.

We all deserve to go to school, and the way we work to make that happen is by each of us taking advantage of our ability to get an education and learn how to make things better around the world.

This is why it's important to learn what you feel passionate and excited about.

You can make the world a better place just by doing what you love!

School is a journey filled with...

HIGHS, LOWS, AND IN-BETWEEN DAYS.

I'd be lying if I told you that you will love going to school every day. (I don't even love going to school every day!)

That's part of life, and school also teaches us how to navigate those days that aren't the best.

A lot of my students decide at a young age that they simply aren't good at something, and won't ever be good at it.

For me, I just see all the years they
have ahead of them to continue
to practice, learn, and grow.

My advice is:

DON'T WRITE YOURSELF OFF SO SOON!

There is plenty of time to build upon your skills and collect knowledge about what you like and what you don't like.

I knew early on that I loved writing and reading but that I had a hard time with math, which sometimes made me feel bad about myself.

Through that challenge, I learned that math probably won't be the thing I do every single day for the rest of my life. And that is OK!

I learned how to

PERSEVERE

and keep trying.

And here's the good news:
you have the ability to do that too!

Going to school means challenges, occasional long days, feeling frustrated, or not always feeling confident.

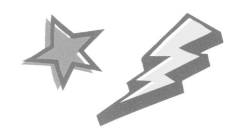

But going to school also means learning, growing, connecting with people, and discovering the special things about you this world really needs.

Do you LOVE...

- Building relationships?
- Caring for the planet and animals?
- Our history as humans?
- Learning about technology?
- Equations which explain how things work?
- Expressing yourself through art and stories?
- Playing sports?
- Being on stage?
- Making new foods?

Don't know yet?
Keep exploring because it's out there.

I HOPE YOU ENJOY THE JOURNEY!

outro

School is something we all need to do, and I hope you're able to see the gigantic value in getting to go to school!

Dear grownup, this is your opportunity to share your thoughts, experiences, and feelings about school. If we are open enough to do this with our kids, they will learn to develop the same skill.

Dear student, remember to keep trying in school (even when it's not always your favorite thing) and keep asking questions. School is an opportunity to learn about yourself and the world around you, so take advantage of it!

Keep talking about school and what matters to you. Keep trying, "failing," and succeeding. It's all worth it because your brain is growing and you are learning!

About The Author

Rachel Burger (she/her) wrote this book for every student who has ever had questions about school or wondered, *What's in it for me?* Throughout her career, she's had many students ask great questions about school—some of which are answered in this book.

Humans are naturally curious, always growing, and love to find the things that call to them. If we can encourage those things in our youngest humans, we can be assured we are using school to our advantage.

This book is meant to provide parents, students, and teachers with a tool to start the conversation about school and learning. It can be difficult to remember all the things we want to say when the opportunity comes up. Rachel's hope is that grownups, parents, teachers, and kids can use this book to start the conversation, and keep it going throughout each kid's learning journey.

 @rachelburgerwrites   🌐 www.rachelburgerwrites.com

a kids book about MONEY by [ ] Stramwasser

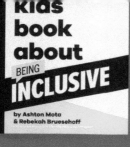
a kids book about BEING INCLUSIVE by Ashton Mota & Rebekah Bruesehoff

a kids book about diversity by Charnaie Gordon

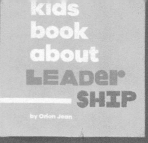
a kids book about LEADERSHIP by Orion Jean

a kids book about IM[ ] by MJ[ ]

a kids book about SAFETY by Soraya Sutherlin, CEM in partnership with JUDY

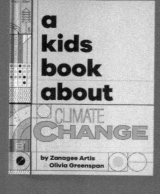
a kids book about CLIMATE CHANGE by Zanagee Artis Olivia Greenspan

a kids book about IMAGINATION by LEVAR BURTON

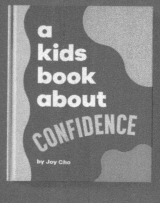
a kids book about CONFIDENCE by Joy Cho

a kids book about Opecia by [ ]on Van

a kids book about NEURO-DIVERSITY by Laura Petix, MS OTR/L

a kids book about racism by Jelani Memory

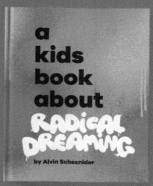
a kids book about RADICAL DREAMING by Alvin Schexnider

a k b a b

a kids book about DIVORCE Ashley Simpo

a kids book about EQUALITY by BILLIE JEAN KING

a kids book about CONSENT by Karli Johnson

a kids book about PRIDE by Kendall Clawson

a kids book about [ ]ame

a kids book about BLENDED FAMILIES

Discover more at akidsco.com

Printed in the USA
CPSIA information can be obtained
at www.ICGtesting.com
LVHW071557301023
762359LV00088B/183